EAST WIND

Modern Day Proverbs and Meditations

by

S.M. Captain

Bloomington, IN  Milton Keynes, UK

authorHOUSE®

AuthorHouse™
1663 Liberty Drive, Suite 200
Bloomington, IN 47403
www.authorhouse.com
Phone: 1-800-839-8640

AuthorHouse™ UK Ltd.
500 Avebury Boulevard
Central Milton Keynes, MK9 2BE
www.authorhouse.co.uk
Phone: 08001974150

First published by AuthorHouse 12/6/2006

ISBN: 978-1-4259-6440-5 (sc)

Library of Congress Control Number: 2006909144

Printed in the United States of America
Bloomington, Indiana

This book is printed on acid-free paper.

Dedication

My Lord and Savior Jesus Christ
Kimberlee Michelle James-Hamilton
I sure do miss you girl
To her babies-D'Andre, KeRon, Kemia, and Robert
Her daddy-Quinton T. Harvey
Her mother-Brenda James
I can still see her in all of you
She would be so proud
To baby E.J.- this lullaby is for you
"I say you're special
But God says you're more
I can give you dreams
But He opens the door
I say you're beautiful
And God says it so
Just who you are
From your head to your toe
You are an angel
You are a king
You are my darling
My little blessing
I love you so much
But He loves you best
Now hush sleepy head
It's time for you to rest"

Acknowledgements

My mother Beulah Baker-Harvey,
You are quite a woman-I love you mom
My husband Amos-You make life sooo good
My children Amos, Ashley, Aaron
I'm proud to be your mother-
My family and friends for all your support and love
To my friend Shirlene-you have always stuck by me, thanks
To Quin, Walter, Nease, Kay, Star, Kris, Stacia and Maggie-
I'm glad you are my family
To Darnell and the whole Richie clan, love you, I can always
count on you to pray for me
To Tina Jones- thanks, you know why
To my Raging Cajuns and Crazy Creoles-Captains, Thomas,
Bolden, love ya
My pastors-Drs. Michael & Bernita Mitchell, thanks for
teaching us the truth
Cornelius and Mae Bertha Johnson-you have earned the god-
parents of the century award, thanks

Preface

"I can not change the world
Only my personal universe
And if I am successful
The world will hear about it"

Dawn...
When revelation comes
To where you are
And releases you
From your obscurity

Courage...
The rage within to persevere anyway
Past fear, doubt and hopelessness
To dream in darkness

Life...
We live by the heart beat of God
Each beat is a summons
Drawing us into the rhythm of His being

Hope…
The oxygen of life

Destiny...
The reason I came
The reason I can't leave until finished

Regret…
When you live in regret
By the time today comes
It's already yesterday

Moments...
Each day is filled with moments
Waiting to be
Embraced, acknowledged, celebrated
That will equal into a lifetime
If given a chance

Blessings...
If you never accept small blessings
You will never be prepared for the greater
Ones

Ashley D. Captain

Constant...
As long as God knows who I am
And I know who I am
I remain
Delivered from
Who man says I am

Adversity...
Gives definition to life in
Character
Connections
Creations

Love…
Is not an ingredient
Nor a potion
It is the blood line of the body
And without it
There is nobody

Living...
Takes confidence
Guts
Creativity
All of which
I came here with

Approval...
Thriving on other's approval
Is like taking a bath in quick sand

Today...
I have a new opportunity to use my faith
To go a little further in my journey
So I think I'll do just that, today

Failure…
Always holds a formula for success
Enlightenment you would never have known
Unless you visited its opportunity

Yesterday...
I may have cried
But today I feel joy
Welling up inside
So tomorrow I know
I'll be all right
This too shall pass

Celebration…
I don't need a joke to laugh
Music to sing
Or a party to celebrate
Me being here is enough

Time…
Time does not sneak up on anyone
It sits quietly waiting
To see what you will do with it

Hope...
Visiting your future with passion
And coming back
With a good report

Passion...
The relentless conviction
To continue despite obstacles

Wholeness...
Is not a condition or a state
It's one decision after another
To move toward
What you already were
Before you came into being

Trust...
Removes the boundaries
So you can see the view
You know existed
Before demolition

Trust...
Enjoying the sunset
Knowing it's going away for a season
And coming back
The next day
To do it all over again

Confidence...
The ability to know your limitations
And then leave them in a cloud of dust

Maturity...
Doesn't come with age
It tag teams with wisdom
And wisdom
Will follow anyone who will listen to it

Elevation...
When your mind is free of all negativity
Although you're walking through rough terrain

Friends...
Those who love you enough to let you transform
And not clip your wings
Because they are of a different color than theirs

Gossip...
Like spending time on the beach
Enjoying the scenery
While sipping on the urine of the passersbyers

Serenity...
Today I speak peace, tranquility,
And quietness into my soul
I pray the God of peace
Guard my heart and mind
And His presence arrest and assures me

Love…
It heals all wounds
It is the smallest sacrifice
With the greatest reward
It visits all yet few know it

Prayer...
Conversation
Between me and God
About my thoughts and His
My concerns and His

Rest...
Relax your grip
Release your hold
Be at ease and still aspire
Allow peace and joy to be restored
Be rejuvenated
Now use hope as your walking stick

Intercession...
The act of giving one's right
To go before God to another
An act of love
That brings your sacrifice of time and love
Face to face with God

God…
Those who say God works in mysterious ways
Haven't gotten to know Him yet

News...
Don't wait for good news
Be good news

Enduring...
Giving up is telling all those blessings that
Have finally caught up with you
You don't want them anymore

Answers...
If I blame all my problems on someone else
Then I must look to someone else for the solution
If I accept responsibility
Then I already have a solution

Help...
The same thing that's meant to help me
Can hurt me if not taken in proper dosage

Appreciation…
Appreciation is not what you do
Or what you say
It is how you live

Thoughts...
Are my private property
But their manifestation
Become everybody's

Love...
Is not a declaration
It is a life long decision

Time...
In between great moments
Are good days
Good hours
Good minutes
Not to be wasted

Sight...
Looking is acknowledging the presence of beauty
Seeing is participating in it

Self-love...
Is giving myself a thorough evaluation
Then taking my own advice
Before I convince myself it's not true

Faith...
Faith is believing
Then going on
Knowing the promise will catch up with me

Feelings...
Will rob you of some of the most wonderful times
Of your life
But truth will escort them back again

Living...
Is not just getting up everyday
It is getting up with an agenda
Written by purpose

Daily...
Each day should begin with the acknowledgment of
God's greatness
Self greatness
And your neighbor's greatness

Direction…
Because He (Jesus) is the
Way, I will always have direction
Truth, I will always be able to decipher
Right from wrong
Life, I must live to the fullest

Battles...
The biggest battle to defeat is self
Not Satan
It's all down hill from there

Forgiveness...
Is removing the noose from your own neck
And destroying the rope before
It chokes the life from anyone else

Patience...
Seeing what I want from a distance
And being o.k. with it

Friendship...
Two people
Many mistakes
More forgiveness
Lots of love

Wisdom...
It is not your ability to open your mouth
That determines your wisdom
But the ability to keep it closed

Success...
Means I get up one more time than I fell down

Disappointment...
Is one step closer to
Your appointment with destiny

Addiction…
Doing the wrong thing repeatedly

Balance...
Knowing I'm not the center of the universe
Even though I am the center of God's heart

Hurts…
Only have the power
I continue to give them
After I have acknowledged them

Envy...
Giving up the right
To enjoy what you have
For the imagination
Of what another does

Guilt...
Paying way too much
For the same thing over and over again

Envy...
Is no green eyed monster
It is a two legged person
With displaced priorities

On-Course...
Even if I don't know the way
Jesus is the way
And as long as I walk in Him
I know I'm on course

Faith...
Faith is allowing your heart
To lead you down roads
Few have traveled

Purpose...
I have not begun to fulfill my purpose until I have
Touched someone else's life

Blame...
I can not blame God
If things aren't right
I can only blame myself
And know He is right
And is willing to help me make things right

Change...
God is the initiator of change
But I only can be the activator

Hairs...
If God has numbered my hairs
I have no right to demand a re-count

Focus...
When I focus on me
My output is one
When I focus on others
My output is innumerable

Dream...
I must take action
While I dream
Lest I wake up and forget

Repetition...
Doing the same thing
Over and over again
Only makes sense if it's living

People...
People are unique
Not perfect

Health...
Health is to be valued
Time invested
And family revered

Relationships...
Relationships should not be disposable
But heat resistant

Destiny...
Destiny is never being afraid
To move on when the time comes

Monuments...
Building monuments does not keep people alive
It's the ones that build them that do

Forgiveness...
The true test of forgiveness
Is being able to help the same people only
With more love than before

Word...
The only difference between
Bless and curse
Is how the Word is handled

Value...
Never allow people to decide your value
Or far too often you'll find yourself with a
Negative balance

Tomorrow...
Tomorrow is within
And can begin any time you decide

Children...
Children can either adorn you with gray
Hairs or laugh lines, it's your choice

Sides...
When taking sides be prepared to stand
Alone because people do get amnesia

Joy...
Joy is only as temporary as I want it to be

Thinking...
The mind can never be left unattended,
Else you will attend to its fruit in the days to come

Play...
Play is relevant to all,
It's only the toys we choose that tarnish the game

Misconceptions...
Getting rid of the misconception that life
Was suppose to be easy makes living, living

Teaching...
You know you have been taught when
The information you have received is now
Creating new information

Stewards...
You don't have children to give them everything
Or expect them to give you everything
They are on assignment just like you,
You are just a temporary steward

Love...
The only instructions love comes with is
"Apply everywhere"

Residency...
It is o.k. to get down
As long as you don't take up permanent
Residence while you're there

Challenges...
Challenges come in different forms and
That can only become a problem when
You conform to the challenges instead of
Allowing the challenge to transform you

Moments...
Life is captivated moment by moment not
By its great events

Worship...
Worship is not a form
It is a quiet reverence within
That knows who is really in charge

Waste...
Waste is a blatant disregard for time and
The favor it gives to us

Peace...
Peace comes from within
From the heart, to the mind and through the body
It is being still when everything else is moving

Friends...
Friends are not suppose to agree to
Everything you say or do, they just agree to
Love you while you work your way through life

Love...
The only way to know true love is to know God
The only way to duplicate this love is to love people

Exhilaration...
The most exhilarating capsules in time is
Letting go
Of those things you don't have control over
And those people who have control over you

Dreams...
When you realize making it is not an option
Dreams have a funny way of coming to you

Success...
Knowing your place is doing your part
Doing your part in excellence is success

Inventory...
If I look around and I have people to depend on
God to trust in
And faith to stand on
I have done well

Wealth...
If I equate success to what I have obtained
Materially, I have failed because who
Determines what enough is
But if I equate success to what I have
Gained spiritually and distributed physically,
I am indeed wealthy

Impact...
It is the imprints that we don't see that
Make the greatest impact

Journey...
When I believe that
Who I am
What I want
And what I need
Is not in some far away distance,
But within me
I have finally begun my journey

Company...
God is with me
I can not be alone

Within...
Finding peace within
Quiets your circumstances

Identity...
Who I am is not the roles I've taken on
It only enhances them

Excuses...
Excuses are the confessions of an
Unconvinced heart

Contents...
(in alphabetical order)

Addiction	58	Excuses	109
Adversity	11	Exhilaration	99
Answers	38	Failure	16
Appreciation	40	Faith	46
Approval	14	Faith	65
Balance	59	Feelings	47
Battles	51	Focus	70
Blame	67	Forgiveness	52
Blessings	9	Forgiveness	78
Celebration	18	Friends	28
Challenges	92	Friends	97
Change	68	Friendship	54
Children	82	God	35
Company	106	Gossip	29
Confidence	25	Guilt	62
Constant	10	Hairs	69
Courage	3	Health	74
Daily	49	Help	39
Dawn	2	Hope	5
Destiny	6	Hope	20
Destiny	76	Hurts	60
Direction	50	Identity	108
Disappointment	57	Impact	104
Dream	71	Intercession	34
Dreams	100	Inventory	102
Elevation	27	Journey	105
Enduring	37	Joy	84
Envy	61	Life	4
Envy	63	Living	13

Living	48	Teaching	88
Love	12	Thinking	85
Love	31	Thoughts	41
Love	42	Time	19
Love	90	Time	43
Love	98	Today	15
Maturity	26	Tomorrow	81
Misconceptions	87	Trust	23
Moments	8	Trust	24
Moments	93	Value	80
Monuments	77	Waste	95
News	36	Wealth	103
On-Course	64	Wholeness	22
Passion	21	Wisdom	55
Patience	53	Within	107
Peace	96	Word	79
People	73	Worship	94
Play	86	Yesterday	17
Prayer	32		
Purpose	66		
Regret	7		
Relationships	75		
Repetition	72		
Residency	91		
Rest	33		
Self-love	45		
Serenity	30		
Sides	83		
Sight	44		
Stewards	89		
Success	56		
Success	101